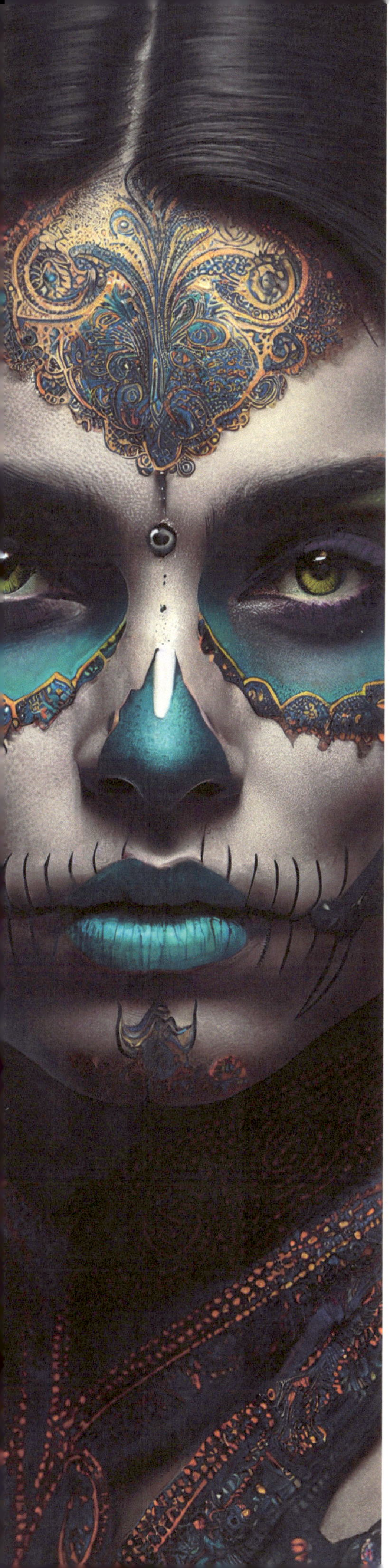

SOULFUL STARES

Immersive Sugar Skull Girl Portraits & Poetry

Welcome to "Soulful Stares: Immersive Sugar Skull Girl Portraits and Poetry," a captivating journey into the depths of enchantment and vulnerability. In this unique book, I explore the mesmerizing world of sugar skull girls, adorned in captivating artistry, drawing our attention to the hypnotic power of their eyes. Through vivid portraits and immersive poetry, explore the intensity and romance sparked by a single gaze. Each poem evokes a sense of wonder, inviting you to embrace the magnetic allure of their eyes and the beauty of the intricate artwork that surrounds them. Prepare to be immersed in a contemporary tapestry of love and art, where the captivating power of a soulful stare ignites emotions and leaves an indelible mark upon your heart.

Sincerly,

Marco Santiago

SOULFUL STARES

Table of Contents

Celestial Embrace

Shadows of Passion

Masquerade of Secrets

Ancient Runes of Desire

Moonlit Pools of Love

Midnight's Enchantment

Melodies in Her Eyes

Reflecting Soulful Love

Palette of Desire

Realm of Dreams

Brushstrokes of Captivation

Tapestry of Love

Constellations of Devotion

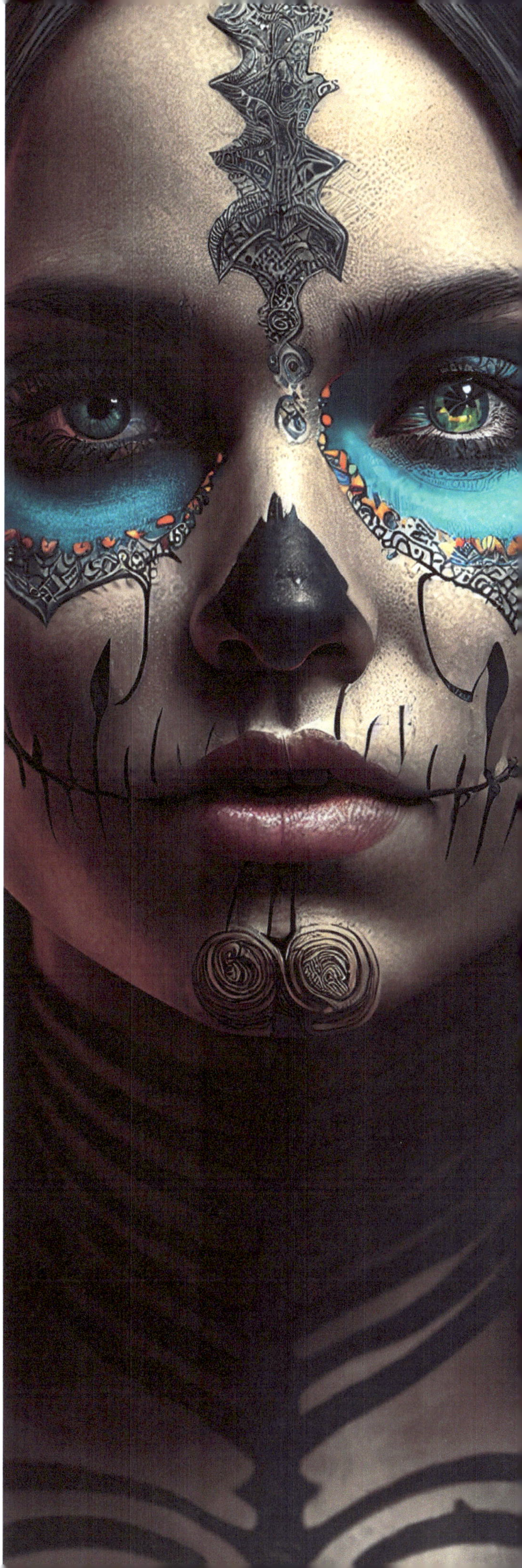

SOULFUL STARES

Immersive Sugar Skull Girl Portraits & Poetry

SOULFUL STARES

Celestial Embrace

In depths of midnight's tapestry, she stands, A sugar skull girl, enchanting and grand. Her eyes, like galaxies, draw me near, A cosmic dance, a love I hold dear. With every blink, a universe unfurls, A kaleidoscope of secrets and pearls. I'm lost within the cosmos of her stare, A celestial journey, beyond compare.

Marco Santiago

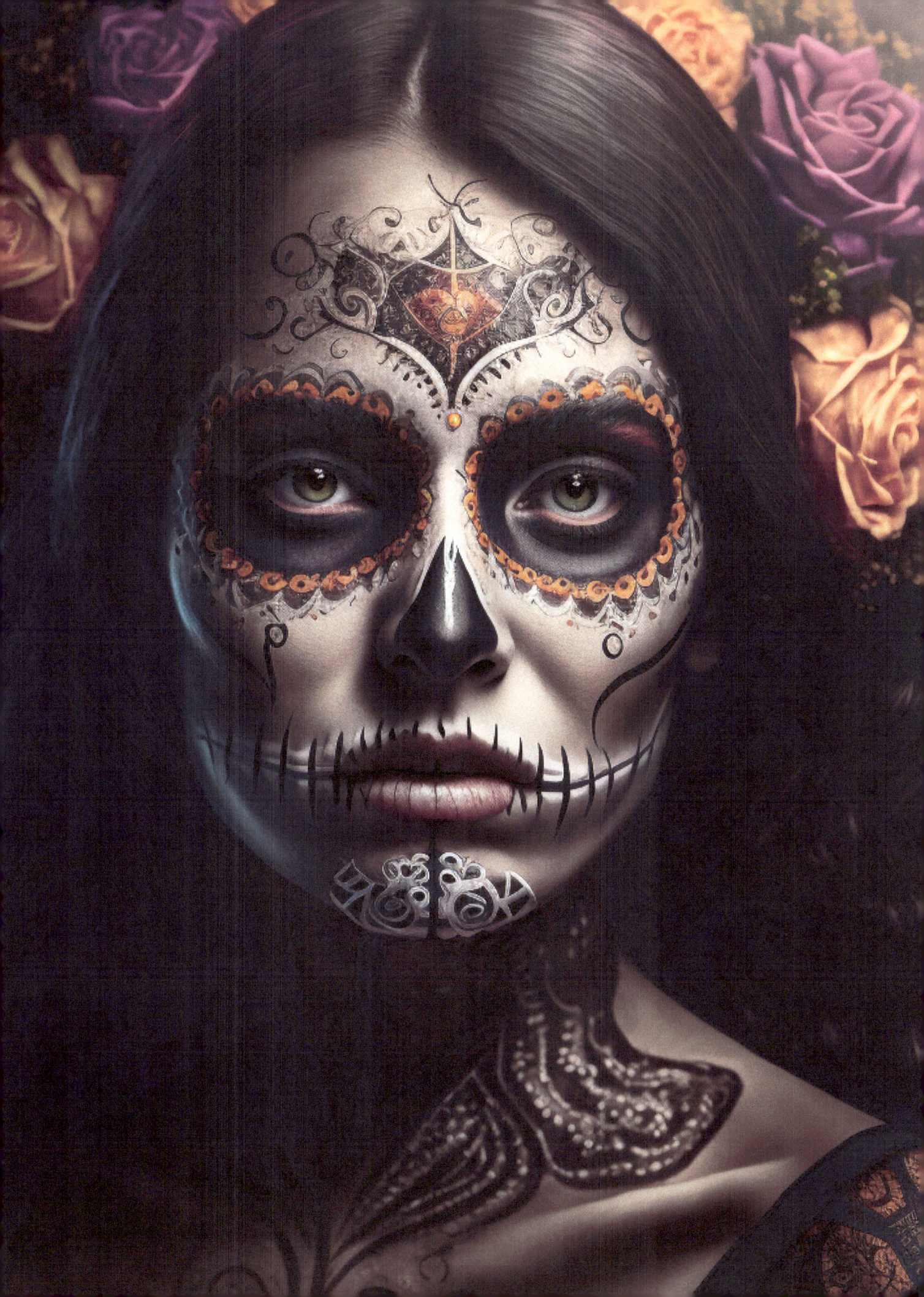

SOULFUL STARES

Shadows of Passion

She paints her eyes with shadows of night, Like stars that shimmer, pure and bright. In their depths, a flicker, a silent flame, Igniting passions I can't help but claim. Her gaze, a portal to dreams untold, A universe where love's secrets unfold. Lost in the labyrinth of her hypnotic stare, I find solace and passion beyond compare.

Marco Santiago

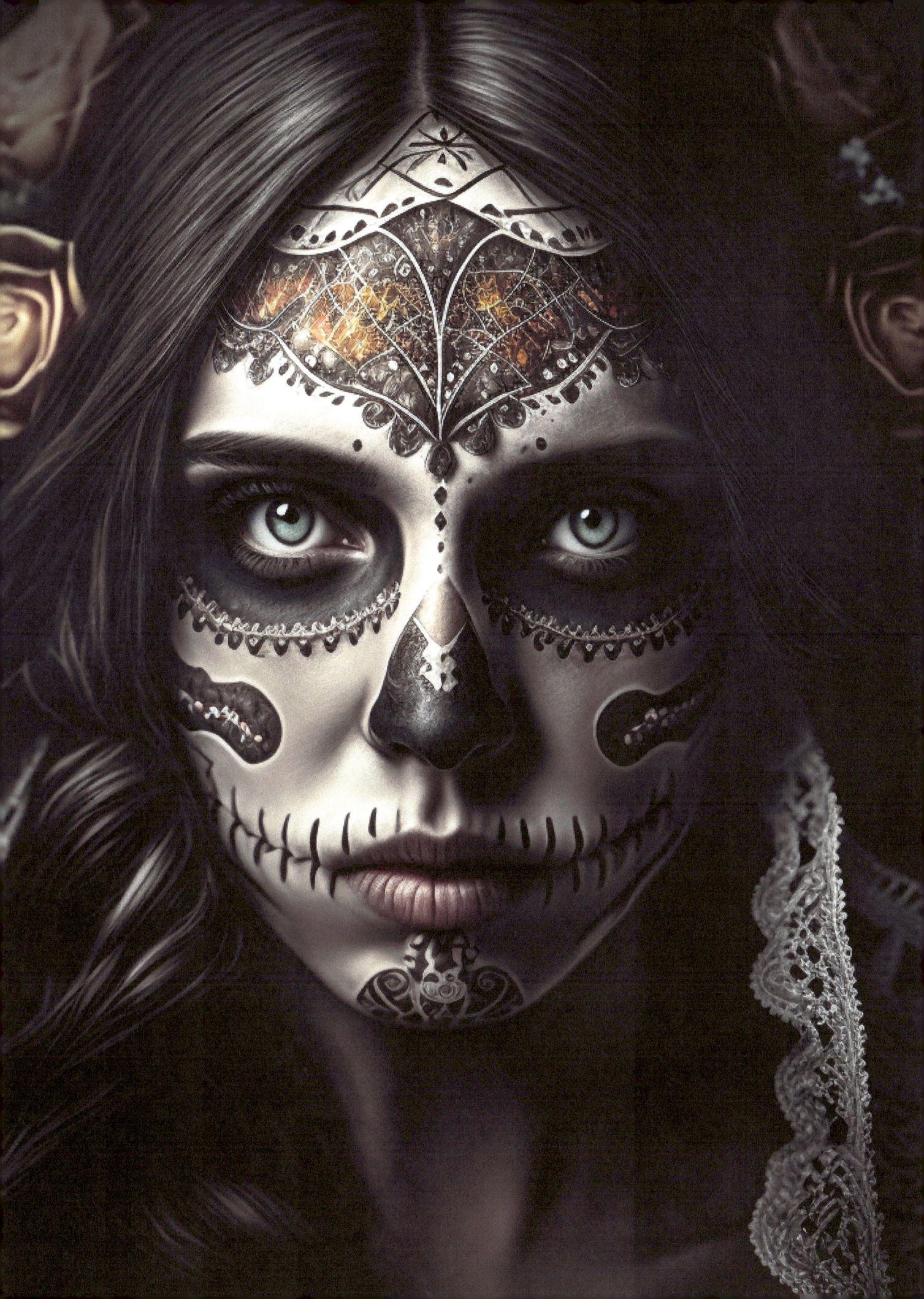

SOULFUL STARES

Masquerade of Secrets

In the masquerade of life, she appears, A sugar skull girl, dispelling my fears. Her eyes, like embers, ignite a fire, Consuming my heart with a burning desire. I'm captivated by her artful grace, As she paints her eyes, a delicate embrace. With each brushstroke, a story unfolds, A love that transcends, forever to hold.

Marco Santiago

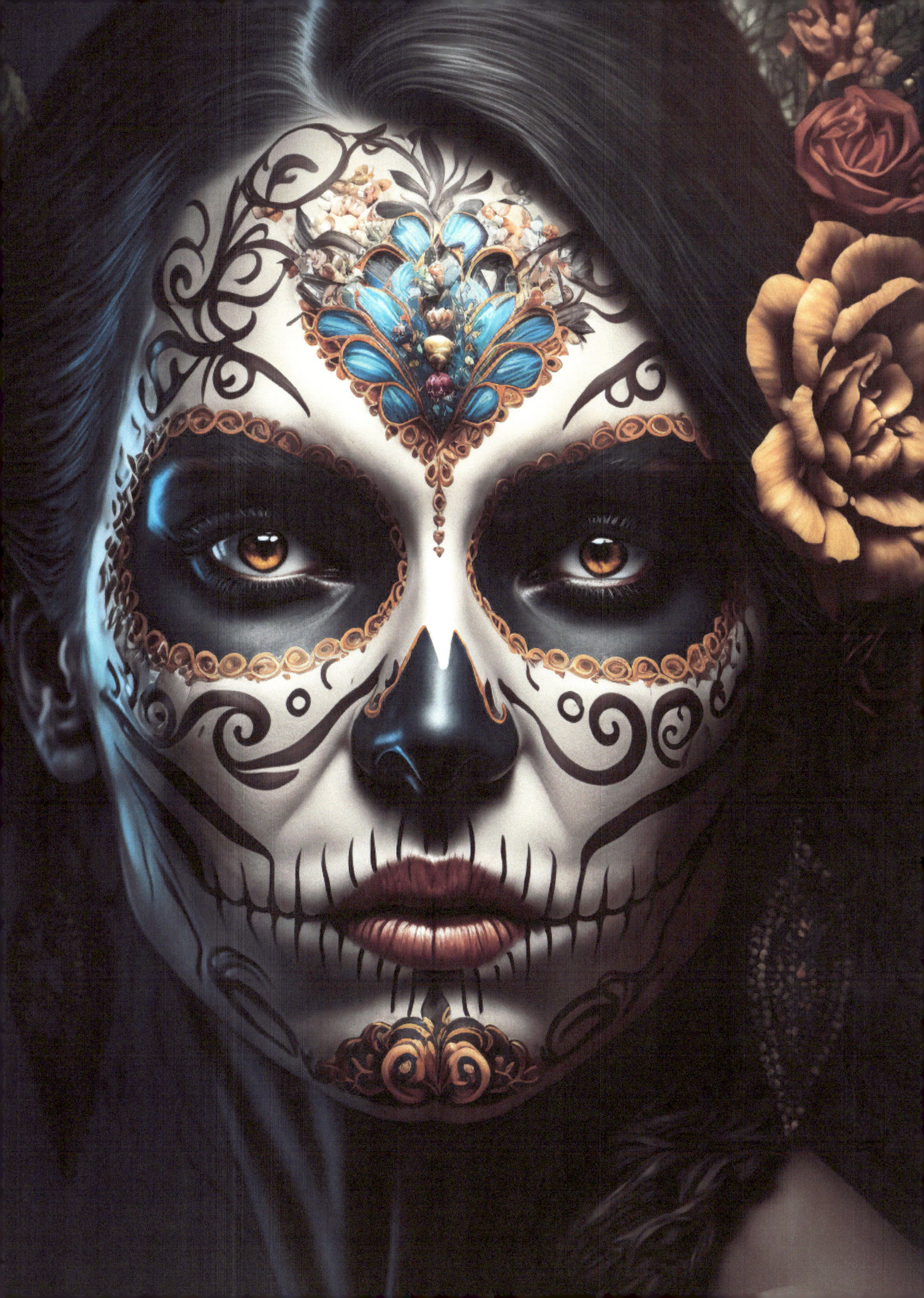

SOULFUL STARES

Ancient Runes of Desire

Her eyes, like ancient runes, speak a tale, A language only the heart can unveil. They hold the secrets of forgotten lore, Whispering promises, forevermore. In their depths, a tempest of desire, A flame that burns, consuming like fire. I'm spellbound, lost in her mesmerizing gaze, A symphony of passion, a love that amazes.

Marco Santiago

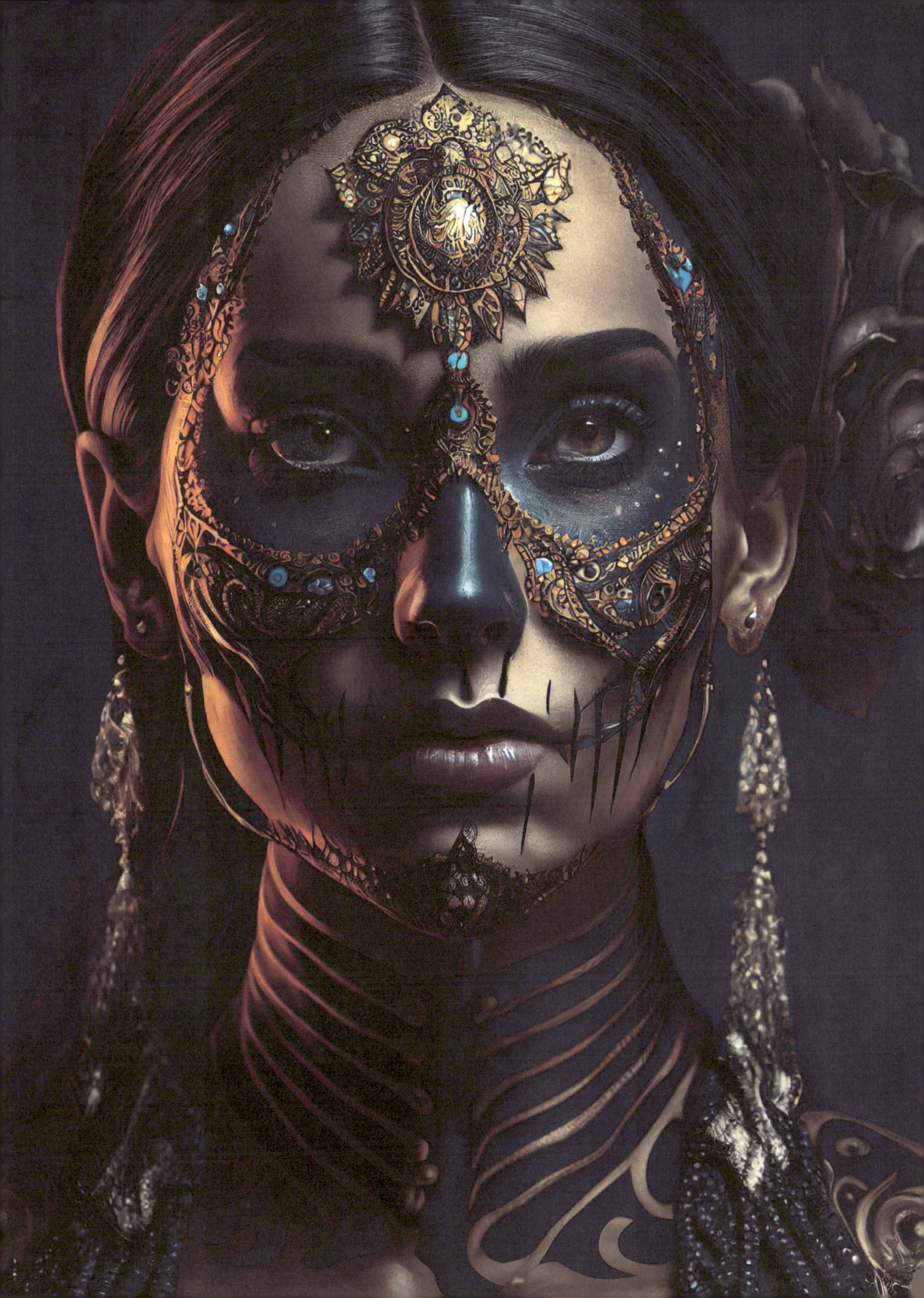

SOULFUL STARES

Moonlit Pools of Love

A sugar skull girl, a vision divine, Her eyes, like moonlit pools, gently shine. Within their depths, a symphony plays, Whispering verses of love's sweet craze. Her eye shadow, an artist's delicate touch, Enhances the emotions, evoking so much. I'm drawn to her like a moth to a flame, Enveloped in her beauty, enchanted by her name.

Marco Santiago

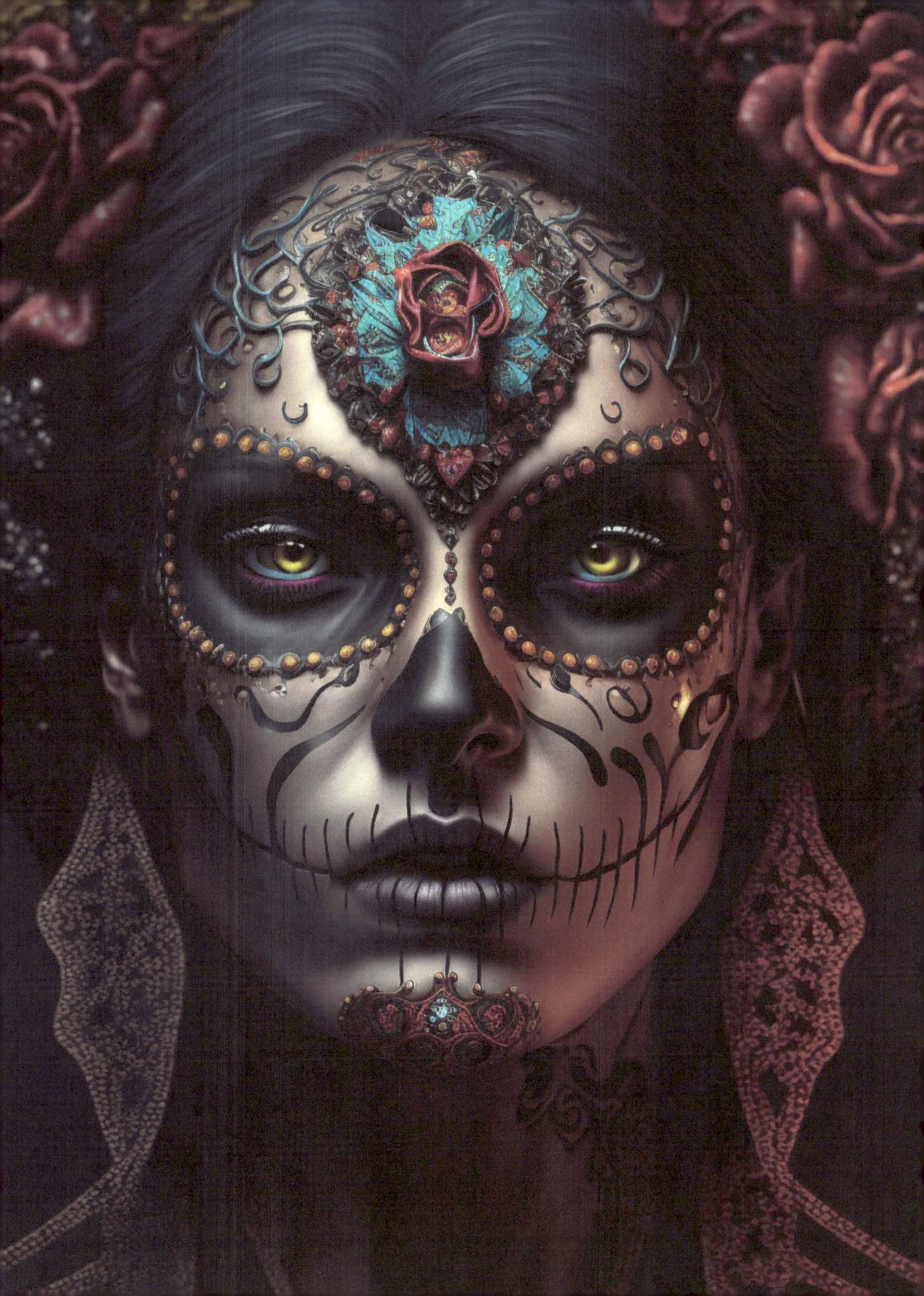

SOULFUL STARES

Midnight's Enchantment

She dons a crown of midnight's embrace, A sugar skull girl with an angelic face. Her eyes, like sapphires, piercing and deep, Hold a promise of love, secrets to keep. In their gaze, vulnerability's trace, A tender connection I can't help but chase. I'm lost in the labyrinth of her captivating eyes, Falling deeper into a love that never dies.

Marco Santiago

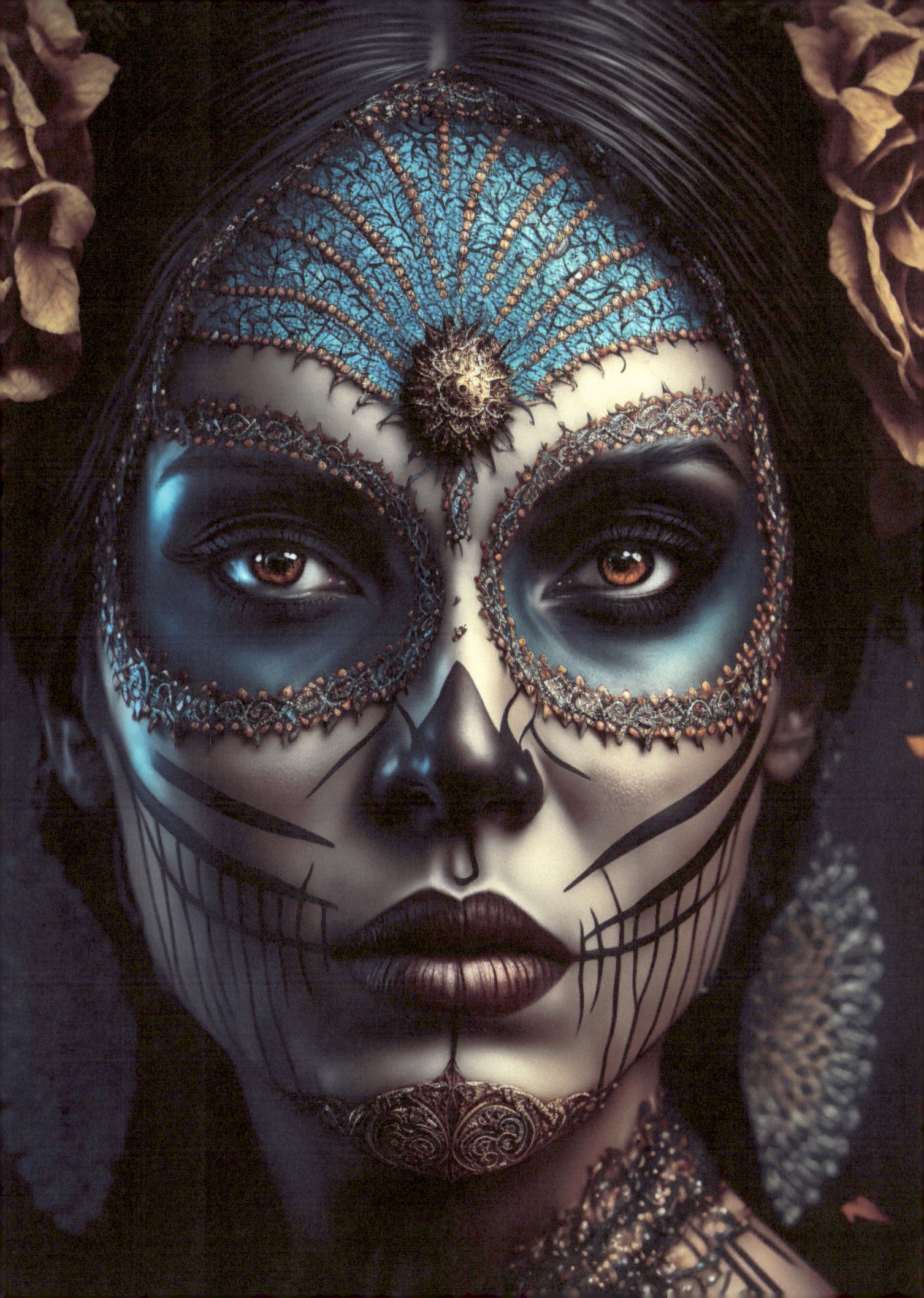

SOULFUL STARES

Melodies in Her Eyes

With every blink, her eyes reveal, A world where fantasies become real. In their depths, a symphony takes flight, Playing melodies of love, day and night. Her eye shadow, an ethereal blend, Draws me closer, my heart on the mend. I'm ensnared by her artful allure, A love so profound, forever pure.

Marco Santiago

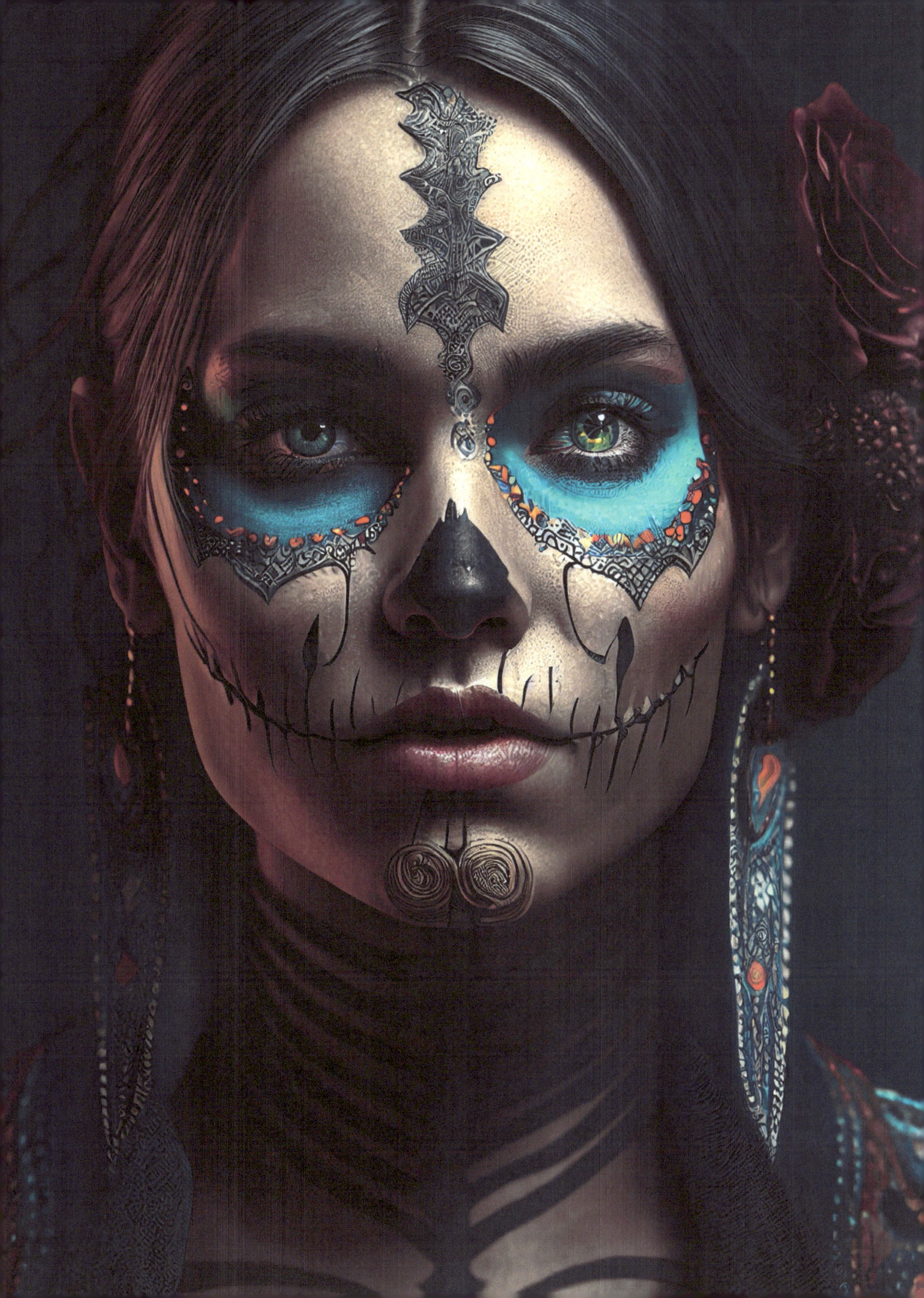

SOULFUL STARES

Reflecting Soulful Love

A sugar skull girl, a vision of grace, Her eyes, like windows, reflect my own face. In their depths, a mirror to my soul, A connection unbreakable, making me whole. Her eye shadow, a brushstroke divine, Paints a portrait of love, a masterpiece to find. I'm enraptured by her hypnotic gaze, Lost in a love that sets my heart ablaze.

Marco Santiago

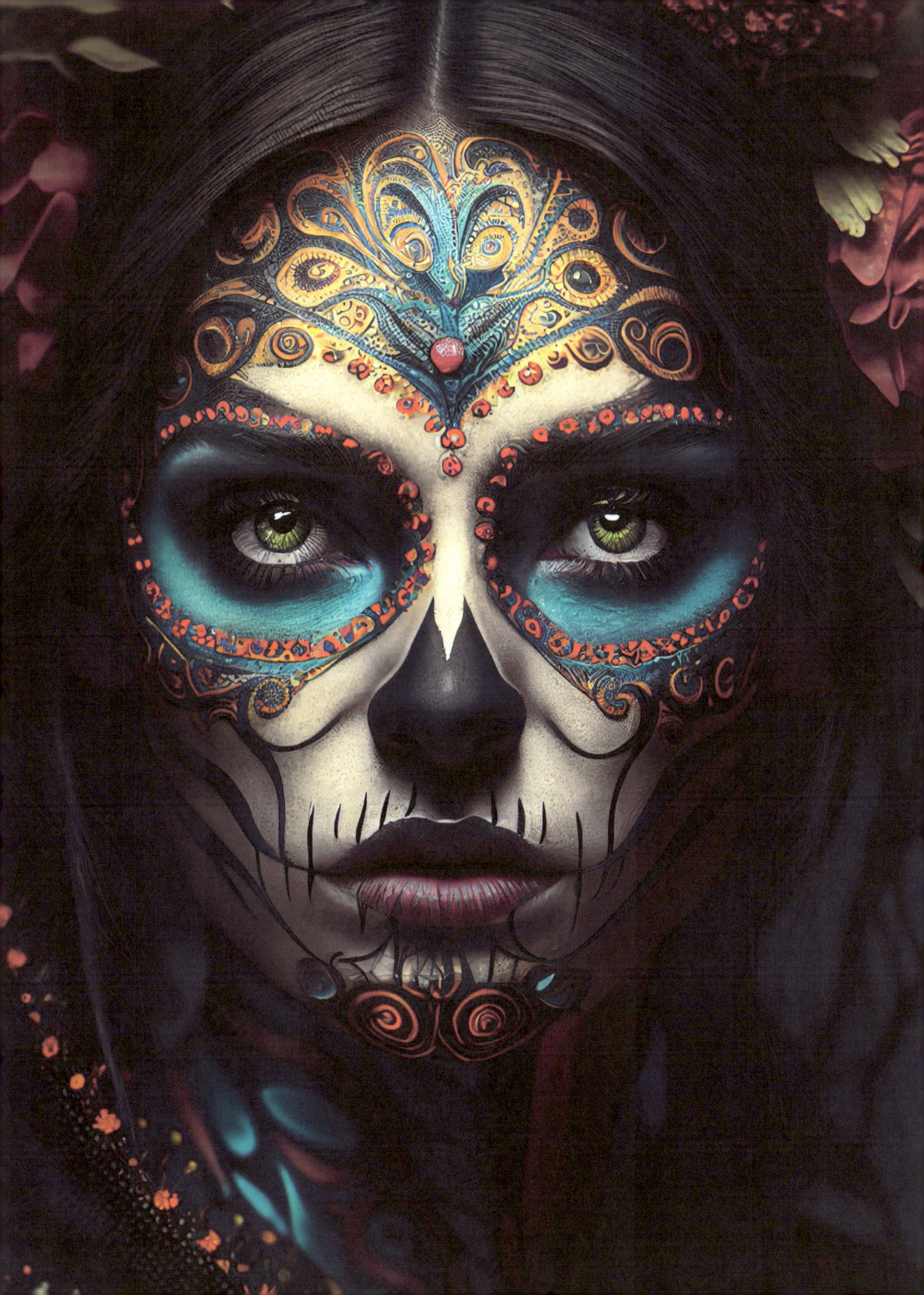

SOULFUL STARES

Palette of Desire

She's a sugar skull girl, adorned in art, Her eyes, like poetry, speak to my heart. In their depths, a sonnet takes shape, Whispering verses, love's secrets escape. Her eye shadow, a palette of desire, Sets my soul aflame, igniting a fire. I'm entranced by her captivating stare, A love so profound, impossible to compare.

Marco Santiago

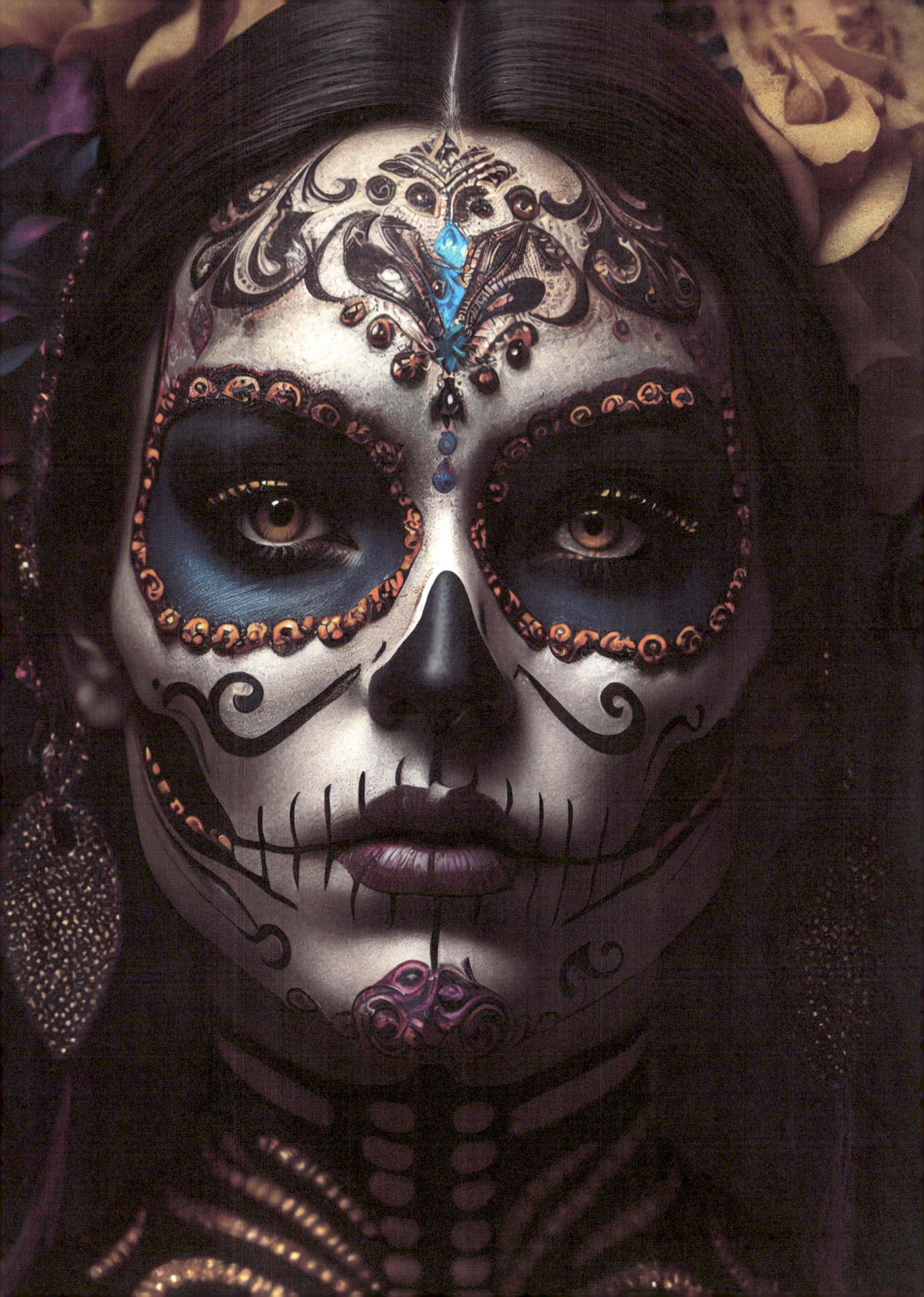

SOULFUL STARES

Realm of Dreams

In the realm of dreams, she weaves her spell, A sugar skull girl, a story to tell. Her eyes, like portals, invite me in, To a world of passion, where love begins. In their depths, a melody softly plays, Guiding my heart through love's intricate maze. I'm enchanted by her magnetic allure, A love so pure, timeless and sure.

Marco Santiago

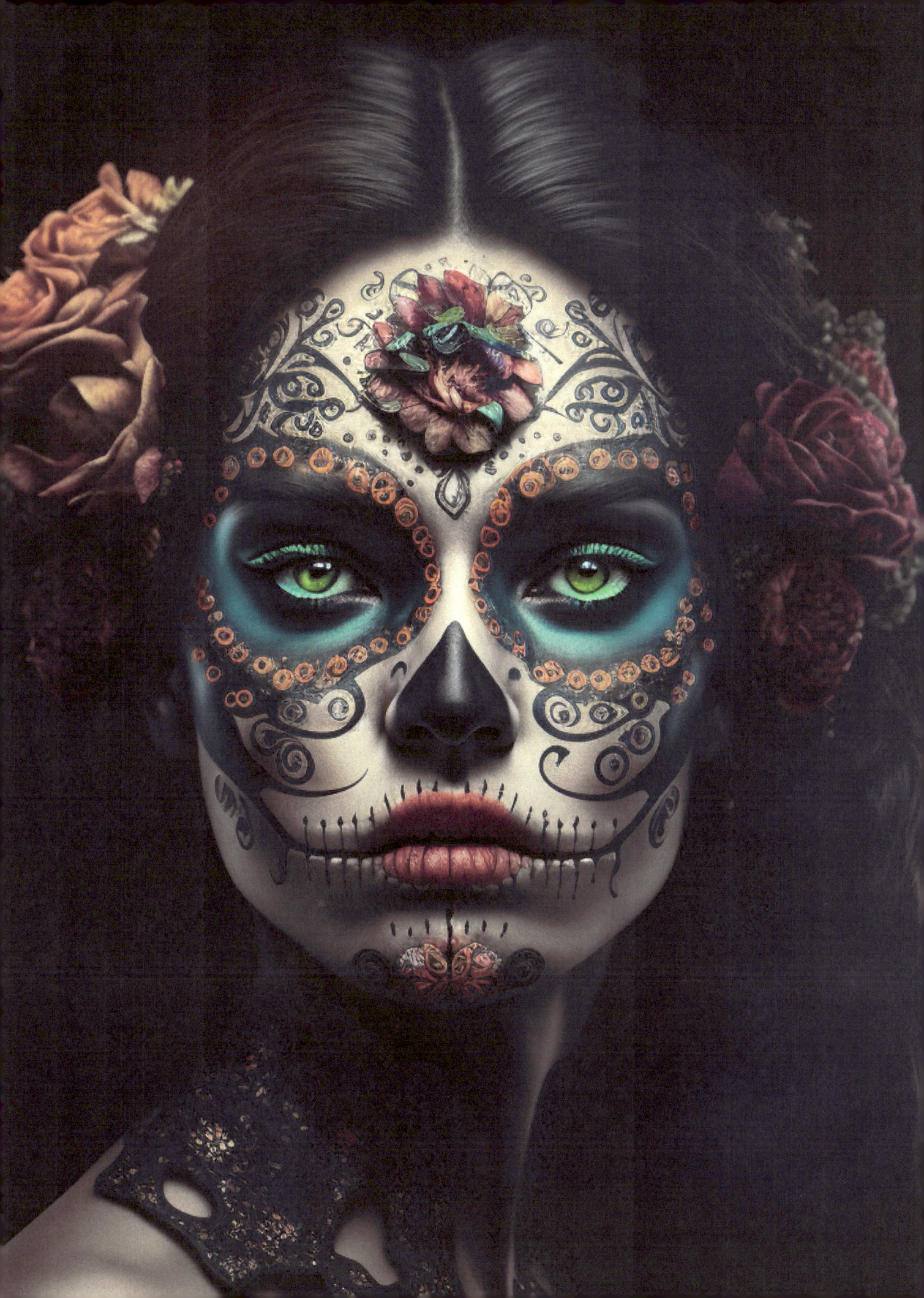

SOULFUL STARES

Brushstrokes of Captivation

She's a sugar skull girl, a masterpiece of art, Her eyes, like brushstrokes, captivate my heart. In their depths, a symphony dances, Inviting me to join, taking love's chances. Her eye shadow, an intricate design, Enhances the emotions, makes them intertwine. I'm mesmerized by her enchanting gaze, Lost in a love that forever stays.

Marco Santiago

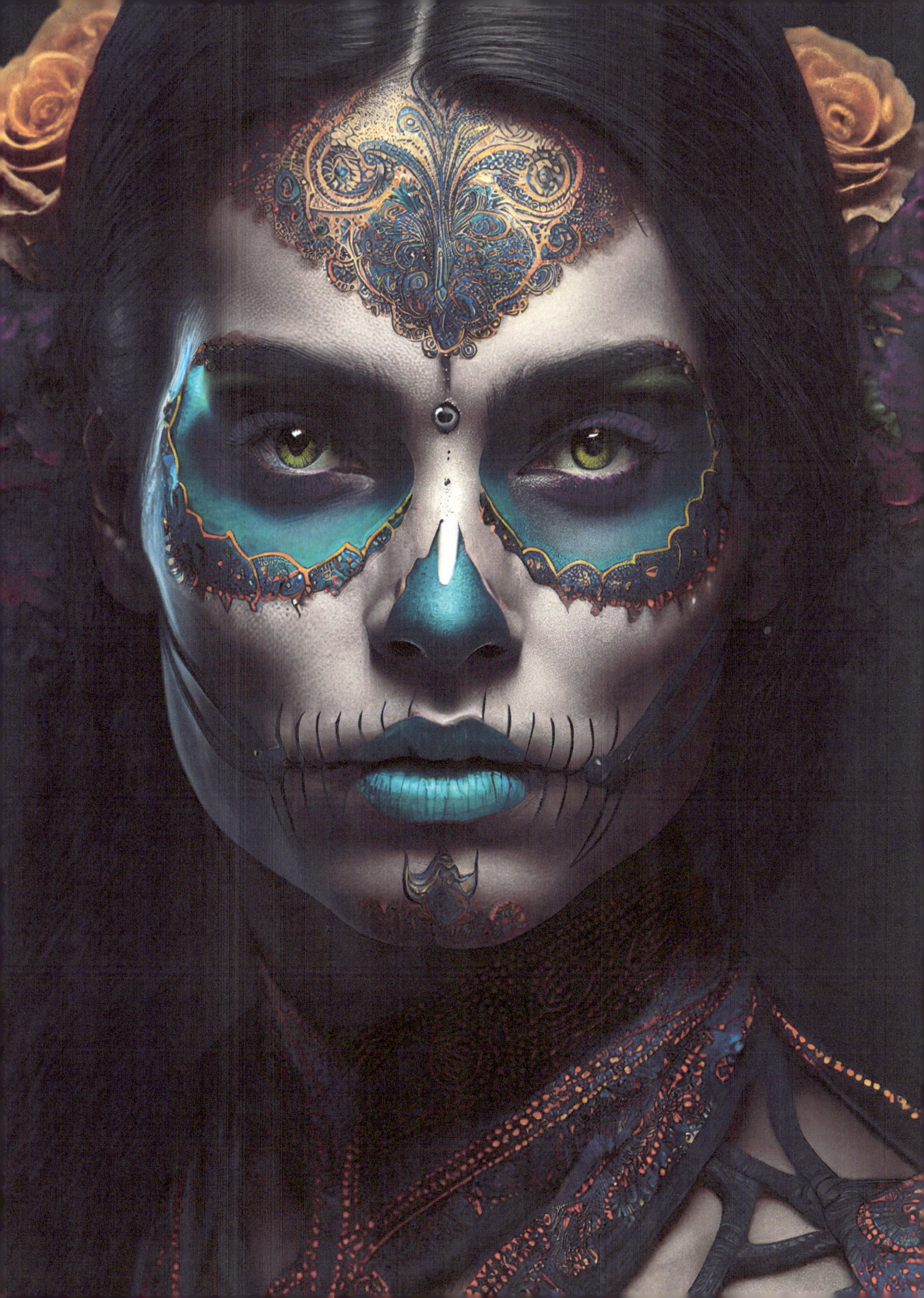

SOULFUL STARES

Tapestry of Love

She adorns herself as a sugar skull queen, Her eyes, like gems, shine with a radiant gleam. In their depths, a story unfolds, A tale of love that forever holds. Her eye shadow, a tapestry of dreams, Invites me closer, bursting at the seams. I'm enthralled by her mesmerizing grace, Bound by a love I'll never replace.

Marco Santiago

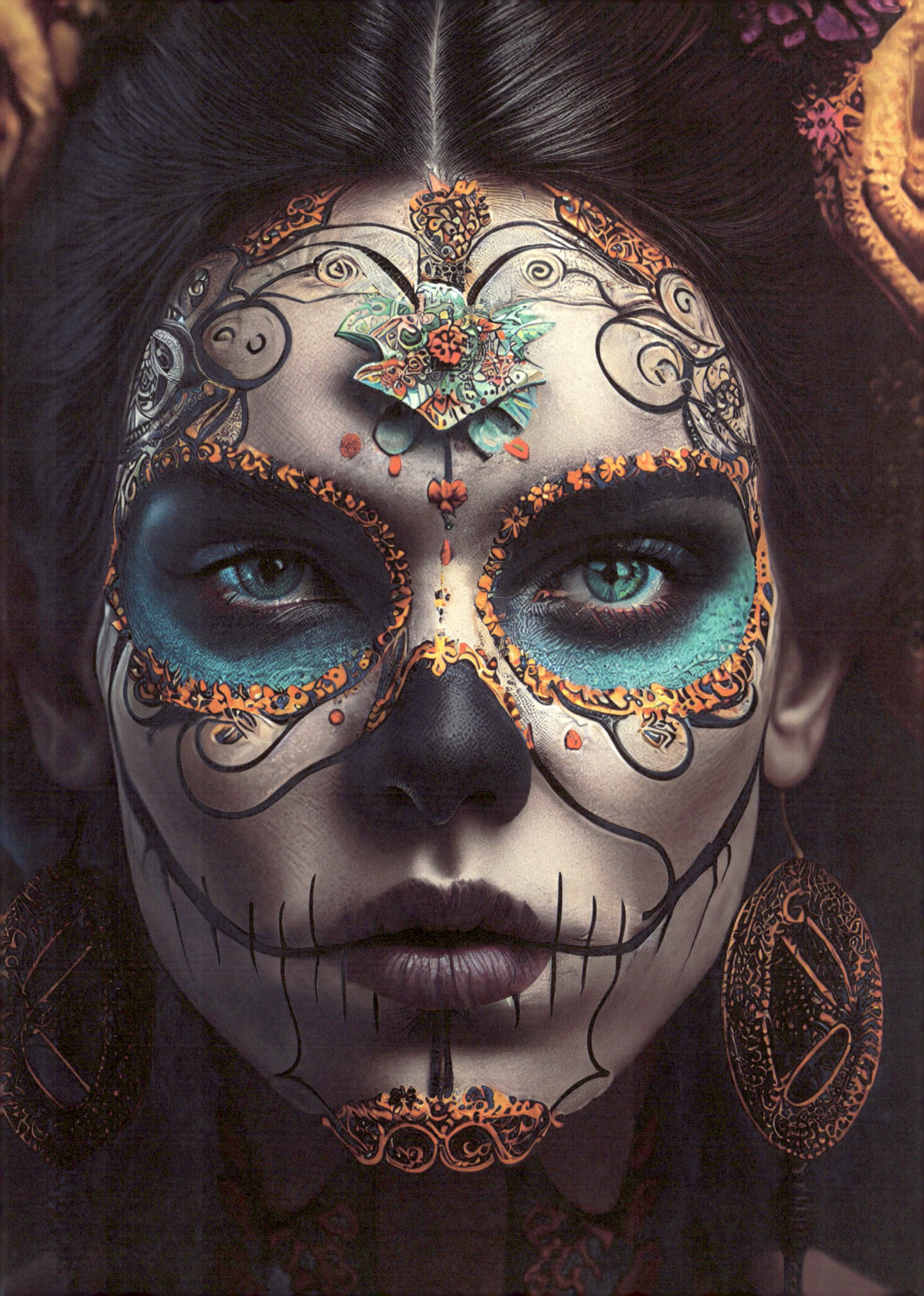

SOULFUL STARES

Constellations of Devotion

A sugar skull girl, an enchantress divine, Her eyes, like constellations, forever shine. In their depths, a universe awaits, A love that transcends, defying all fates. Her eye shadow, an artist's creation, Enhances the emotions, fuels the sensation. I'm spellbound by her captivating art, A love that ignites, eternally in my heart.

Marco Santiago

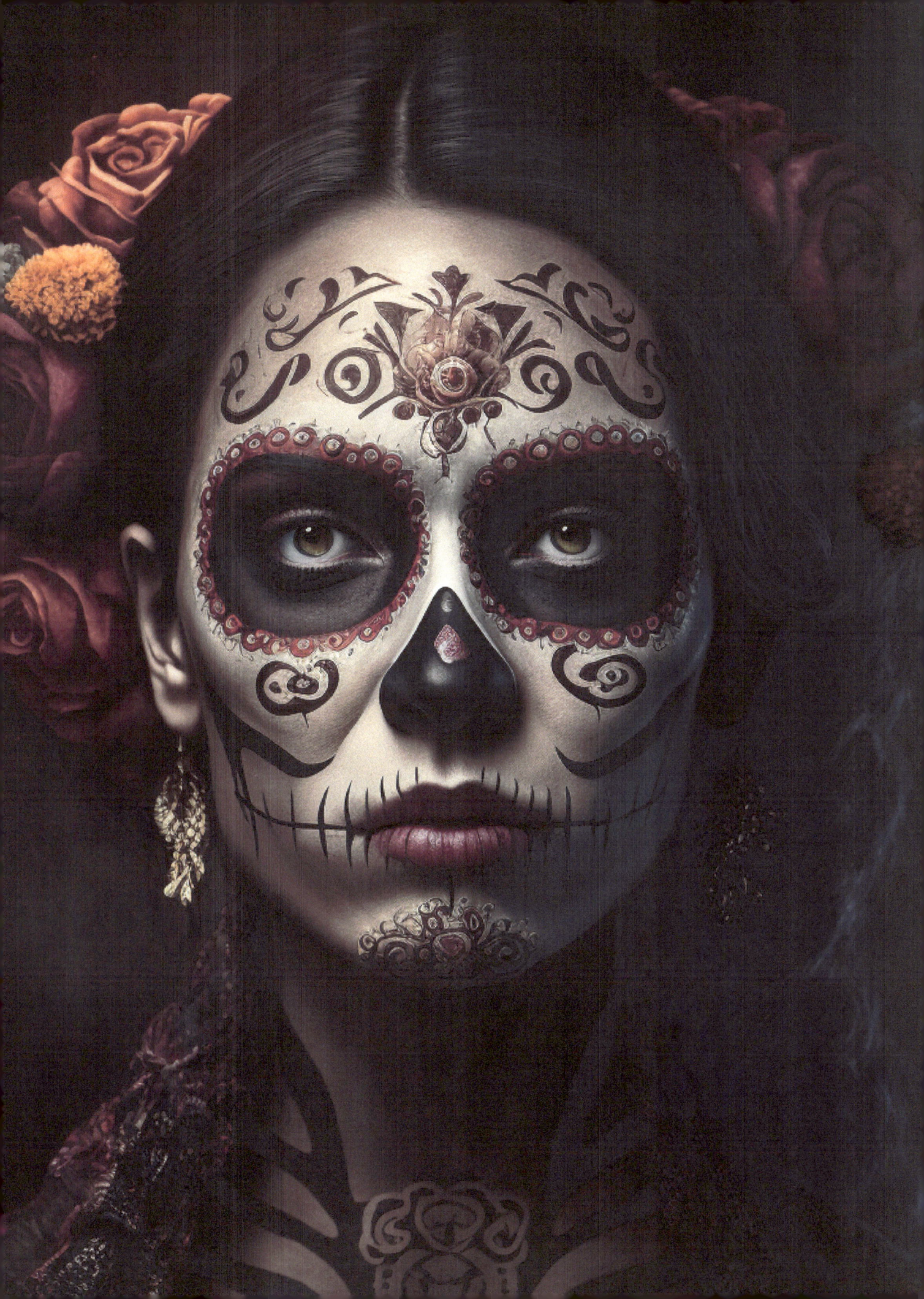

The End.

SOULFUL STARES

Immersive Sugar Skull Girl Portraits

Dear Reader,

I extend my deepest gratitude and heartfelt appreciation for embarking on this journey through "Soulful Stares: Immersive Sugar Skull Girl Portraits and Poetry." Your presence and support mean the world to me.

Thank you for opening your heart and mind to the captivating and engaging world I've strived to create within these pages. It has been my sincerest desire to transport you to a realm of enchantment, where vulnerability and intensity intertwine, and the power of a single gaze becomes a catalyst for romance and introspection.

Your willingness to explore the magnetic allure of these sugar skull girls, their mesmerizing eyes, and the artistry that surrounds them is truly inspiring. It is my hope that you have been immersed in a world where emotions run deep and where the power of poetry and imagery intertwine to awaken the senses. Your support as a reader fuels my passion to continue weaving tales that evoke both emotion and imagination. I am deeply grateful for the opportunity to share this artistic journey with you.

Once again, thank you for joining me on this enchanting adventure. Your presence has made it all the more special, and I hope that "Soulful Stares" has left an indelible mark upon your heart.

With heartfelt appreciation,

Marco Santiago